SECRETS OF
TUTORING SUCCESS

Creating a Tutoring
Business You
(and Your Students)
Will Love

Patrick Clancy

STRATFIELD STRATEGIC SOLUTIONS, LLC

For my students. Never stop learning.

CONTENTS

PREFACE

My first tutoring experience was not what I expected. A young man around 20 years old reached out to me, asking for help with his college-level financial accounting class. I met him in the lobby of a hotel not far from my home and for the next two hours I reviewed all of his class materials with him. The following night, we had a second session to prepare for his exam. At the end of the session, the student said, "You are really good at this. How long have you been tutoring?" He was just as surprised as I was to find out it was my first client experience! I was happy, the student was happy, and my bank account was happy.

Over hundreds of students and thousands of tutoring hours later, I was being asked different questions, this time from others wanting to start their own tutoring businesses. Many have asked, "How did you get started," "How do you find students," "How do you know what to charge?" These are just some of the many questions I answer in this book.

Whether you are just starting out, or if you are an established tutor looking to develop your business, this book will walk you through all you need to know.

After a few years of tutoring, I asked my own question... "How can I help others create successful tutoring businesses?" The answer is this book!

It is my hope that you find your tutoring experience as fulfilling as I have.

Tutor On!

NOTES ABOUT THIS BOOK

To provide you a high likelihood of accomplishing your goals utilizing this book, the following are some notes to ensure this is the right book for you, and some helpful remarks to consider as you use it:

Depending on your geographic location, terms might be slightly different. Generally, I refer to the person being tutored as the student, whereas others may refer to them as the "learner," "tutee," or perhaps a "client."

I switch usage of the term "student" to "client" when dealing with business matters. It is your student who learns, it is your client who pays you. These can be the same physical being, but your relationship with them can, and generally will, be different.

Similarly, the term "tutor" is used as a reference to the person providing guidance, knowledge, instruction, or insight to the other party. Many tutors are also "instructors," "coaches," "mentors," "teachers" etc.

In my opinion, there is a difference between a "teacher" and a "tutor," although I have colleagues that may dispute this. Generally, I believe that "teaching" is the first time the material is presented to the student. The second and subsequent instances of presenting the material to the student are usually done both by a tutor and a teacher.

If you are consistently the first party to present material to students, you may also want to consult a teaching methods textbook since the primary delivery of content is different than the second and subsequent delivery of material.

This book is written to apply to tutors working with students of all ages, demographics, and ability levels. There are certain sections that may pertain more to those tutoring students of college age and beyond and those working with students in primary and secondary school settings.

Finally, this book is primarily intended for tutors working outside of corporate organizations. (e.g. a Kaplan, Pearson, Huntington, etc.) Those organizations typically have their own set of policies, materials, and locations that a tutor will be required to operate within. However, tutors working at these corporate locations may benefit from some of the tips and techniques discussed in the book.

PART ONE

ORGANIZING YOUR BUSINESS

Understanding Your "Why"

If you are reading this book, you clearly have some interest in being a tutor. Perhaps you have already started and want to expand your current business or maybe you do not even know where to begin. Regardless, before going further, it is critical to understand your why. Why do you want to tutor? Are you an experienced professional who wants to share their knowledge? Do you enjoy working with students who have learning challenges, or you want to give back to a community that has provided opportunities to you personally?

There are many reasons why people tutor. Some of these include:

- Sharing professional experience with students

- Seeing others succeed in their academic, athletic, or musical pursuits

- Earning money (either as a full-time job or part-time income)

- Giving back to their community, school, or institution

- Staying sharp on subjects and up to date on new material

While you may be tempted to skip this exercise, let me explain why it is critical to understand your why.

Your why will determine:

- What students you seek to tutor (age, subjects)

- What you will (or will not) charge for your expertise

- Where you will acquire your students

- How often you will tutor

- What you seek to gain from tutoring

Take the next few minutes to write down two or three reasons why you want to tutor, who and what you intend to impact, and how you will determine your success. Keep these reasons saved in a location where you can refer to them later. You will see the importance of these reasons both later in the book and in your tutoring adventure.

First Steps

Now that you know why you are going to tutor, it is time to decide what subject(s) you are going to offer. It is likely that you have already thought of a few topics. When first starting out, limit the number of subjects you offer until you gain traction in those areas. Answer the questions below to help narrow your scope. Note that this does not mean you cannot change these subjects later or are only going to work within these bounds. This is merely a starting point to progress from. Write these subjects down so you can refer to them later as your business expands. In a future chapter, I will have you refer to this list.

- What is the age range of students you intend to focus on? Elementary through high school students (and specifically what grade range), college students, adults, seniors?

- What subject(s) do you intend to focus on? Be specific. If you say "math," what type of math are you focusing on (geometry, algebra, calculus)? The more specific you are, the better matches you will have with potential students. Write down all possible subjects even if they seem duplicative. Many students are searching for specific experience and expertise and will pay extra for it.

- At what level do you plan to offer services (e.g. AP classes or only introductory courses)? For example, if you are planning on tutoring Microsoft Excel, you might only be skilled up to a certain level. It is important to honestly assess your abilities before reaching out to potential clients (more about that in the next section).

- You should assess if what you want to tutor is practical based on the circumstances. This is particularly relevant to tutors of physical activities. For example, if the subject you plan on tutoring requires specialized equipment or other materials, make sure you have or can obtain these.

Qualification

Once you have picked your target age range, topics, and skill level you are going to focus on, you may be tempted to skip forward and find your first student. However, before you start tutoring you must consider if you are qualified to tutor the topic or topics you plan on working with students.

Sometimes qualification is not a hard and fast rule. Let me explain:

- Depending on the subject you are tutoring, you may need a certification or permission to claim expertise. Example: you are claiming to be an "Expert SAT Tutor utilizing Company ABC's materials." If you do not have ABC company's permission to utilize their name (and in some cases their materials), you could find yourself in trouble.

- Some tutoring sites have their own qualification tests, as do many tutoring service providers and companies. Tutoring service providers may require a college degree or professional experience. In some cases, your prior experience in a teaching discipline or work experience may be substituted for these qualification exams. Of course, if you are certified in anything, it is always worth highlighting to potential students.

- Most important: Tutors should always review class materials, textbooks, syllabi, and practice or prerequisite assignments PRIOR to engaging in a session with a student. It is the tutor's responsibility to ensure they are both comfortable and capable of adequately explaining the materials to the student.

Please, take this last point seriously. I cannot count the number of times a student has come to me saying, "I had a session or two with another tutor, but they did not really understand the material." This is a waste of the student's time (and perhaps money). It is maddening enough for a student to not understand something...they do not need another reason to be frustrated.

It is perfectly acceptable to decline a request for tutoring in a subject area, or at a level of experience/expertise you are not comfortable with. Your students (and those you declined) will thank you.

Tutoring Must Haves

What you need to start your tutoring business depends on the way you plan to tutor: in-person or online. If you plan on doing a mix of both, consider how much time you plan to utilize potentially costly items such as rental space and other resources.

In-Person Tutoring

Here are some things you will likely need if you are conducting tutoring in-person:

- Space: This refers to the physical location where you plan on conducting your tutoring.

- If you are meeting clients in person, you will want to have a place (or places) where you can conduct your sessions effectively. It is important to have a quiet space with a solid internet connection for research or if the student's work is online.

Tutoring at Your Home

- The tutoring space should be clean, well-lit, and provide enough space for you and your student to spread all materials out without feeling cramped.

- If possible, the tutoring location in the home should be in a separate room, such as an office or library, to avoid distractions. If you have family members or pets at home during tutoring sessions, any noise should not be heard within your tutoring space. Basements and studios above garages are also possibilities, assuming they are well lit and climate controlled.

- If you are tutoring students who have a parent or other person with them, provide a space for them to sit as well. Generally, it is best to conduct your lessons without anyone else present to encourage focus, however, your student (and their parent/guardian) must be comfortable with this. You should refer to the "Difficult Situations" chapter in this book for more on this topic.

- Provide your clients with a place to park as well as an area to leave their shoes, jackets, backpacks, etc.

If you have not realized by now...the kitchen table next to your barking dog is NOT the place to tutor out of your home!

One other note about tutoring out of your home - Some cities, towns, or counties may require a special business license or permit to conduct business out of a home. I go into detail about this topic in the section "Are you setting up a business?" You may want to consult local laws and regulations to see if a permit may be necessary.

Other Locations

- The local library: The library study room is a convenient, free, and usually an accessible place to meet students. You and your student may need library membership or local residency for this to work. Also, you will need to have permission to connect to the internet at the library if your sessions require it.

  - **Caution!** Be careful not to exchange money or advertise your services in the library without permission. While it may be free to use, most libraries prohibit business activities or promotions.

- Schools: Public and Private schools may have rules prohibiting tutoring for compensation. You should inquire about this ahead of time. If you are tutoring free of charge, make sure you are allowed to enter the school grounds before setting up an appointment.

- College or University: For students in higher educational settings, there may be study spaces on campus that the student can reserve.

- Coffee Shops: I have a love-hate relationship with coffee shops. While it is generally free to conduct business there (I recommend you buy something if you are using their facility), the Wi-Fi is unreliable. Also, some coffee shops have music playing or lots of customers coming in and out which can be distracting. I have also run into situations where there was no table available for a lesson.

- Student's Home: If visiting a student's home, use the same protocol as you would in your own home. This means asking the student what type of workspace they have available to them. Propose an alternative if it seems like there may be too many distractions.

- Other possible locations that might work: Churches, community centers, and apartment community rooms.

Places I Do Not Recommend

- Restaurants, bars (for obvious reasons)

- Outdoor spaces

- While traveling, at a hotel, or on an airplane or train where the internet is generally unreliable

- Dorm rooms, as there is not enough space and it may feel awkward

Materials for In-Person Tutoring

- Paper, pens, pencils, calculators, rulers, and other "must haves" for the subject you are tutoring. This can get expensive for certain subjects (chemistry etc.) and you may need to consider this when setting your price (more about that later on).

  o If your student needs it, you should have it!

- Laptop and internet passwords, if needed

- Textbooks, copies of assignments

  o You may be able to find books from the local library or online for free or at a very low cost. There are even some libraries with test prep material. Just make sure not to write in them or make photocopies unless permitted.

  o If you are regularly printing assignments, it is worth keeping extra printing supplies such as paper and ink on hand. Running out at the last second is not ideal.

- Anything else to make the lesson as hands-on and interactive as possible.

- A watch or wall clock: do not use your phone. Yes, your phone has a clock on it, however, the temptation to look at your phone for reasons other than the time is too great. Instead, set your phone to silent or "emergency" mode if there are certain people that always need to reach you. It is extremely rude to a client if you are constantly checking the time. Eventually, you will get a "feel" for how much time has gone by based on the subject and the student you are working with. If you constantly find yourself running over, set the vibration mode on your phone or smart watch a few minutes before the end of the session to wrap things up.

Online Tutoring

- A reliable and fast internet connection is a must. Before conducting your first lesson, you should perform a speed test to make sure that you can use the applications you will be relying on during your tutoring session. Do not count on coffee shop Wi-Fi to support the sharing of audio, video, or screens. If you are working from home, you should test the speed while others are using the internet and their devices are connected and operating. This is especially important if others in the home are using large bandwidth devices such as gaming platforms or music and video streaming.

- Obtain a good pair of headphones with a noise canceling microphone so that any small background noise disruptions will not be picked up.

- A secondary monitor is critical. This is extremely helpful when sharing your main screen and you need to reference documents on the other, or you have answers on one screen while your student is solving a problem on the other.

- In terms of noise, establish that you are in a quiet place and disruptions are minimized.

- For tutors who are making this their full-time business, it may be worth looking into a power-backup generator, especially if you are in an area where the power goes out frequently.

- You should have the ability to "tether" a mobile phone to a computer in case of an emergency when the internet is out.

- A good desk and chair as well as a wireless mouse and keyboard will provide better comfort for you during longer sessions. If you plan on working multiple hours in front of your computer, these items will make a huge difference.

Other Materials for Online Tutoring

If you are tutoring online (even if it is only part of your business) the following items will provide a reliable experience for you and your students:

- A laptop with a built-in webcam, adequate storage (file) space, a built-in wireless adaptor, and up-to-date security and applications.

- A modern modem and wireless router with built-in security.

- A hard-wire backup in case the wireless is slow since a hard-wire connection is usually faster and more stable.

- Video conferencing software such as Zoom, GoToMeeting, Microsoft Teams or WebEx (among others), if you are not using a partner service that offers their own software or platform.

  o Many of the listed programs have free and paid versions, with the main difference being the number of participants that can be in the meeting simultaneously. If you plan on holding sessions with two or more students, consider purchasing the program rather than using the free version.

- Extra batteries, keyboard and mouse, and power cords.

- Paper, pens, and pencils (you may find taking notes on hard copy paper to be easier than switching between screens).

- Desk lighting to ensure you can see your work surface and participants can see you.

- A whiteboard or sketchpad to draw images on that can be sent to your student.

- An external hard drive is a good idea to periodically backup your files.

- Screen recording software if your students may want a recording of your sessions, or if you may want to review your own lesson notes later.

Pro Tip: Solution Packs. There are a variety of websites that offer textbook solutions (some free, some paid). Be careful as some sites are better than others! While a tutor should generally be able to solve any problem that is asked by the student, sometimes even tutors need a little help. These solutions can also provide other solution-solving steps that can be used to guide the student. In addition to these websites, many textbooks have solution manuals that can be purchased, or teacher editions that contain solutions and other problem-solving methods.

Going Solo or Signing Up with a Service

As discussed in the intro, the primary focus of this book is for tutors operating independently of corporate tutoring services. However, there are several services that connect students and tutors through independent contractor agreements. These agreements generally state that while the service will facilitate connections between students and tutors, you are not an employee of their company. Many of these providers will send you a 1099 (U.S. tax form) at the end of the year and will not withhold taxes.

We will discuss this type of arrangement with the title of "signing up with a service." A quick internet search will help identify some of the major service providers in this space.

Working on your own provides a great list of benefits, but there can be challenges. To review, we will discuss a pro and con list:

Pros of Working by Yourself:

- Retaining 100% of your fee (many sourcing services charge administrative fees)

- No minimum hour requirement (some sites may want you to commit to a specific number of hours per week or month)

- Tutor where, when, and how you want (use whatever means and methods you like)

- No limitation on materials, structure of lessons, or session duration

- Work with the students you want for as long or short as you want (you can end the relationship without a reason or justification)

Cons of Working by Yourself:

- It can be harder to source clients (especially when starting out)

- You are responsible for collecting payments (some services provide payment collection services)

- Requires access to digital tools if you are working online

- Disputes and disagreements must be managed directly rather than through a third party

I generally recommend going solo if you are a tutor focused on tutoring students 18 and under (e.g., elementary through high school). This way, you can advertise locally and source clients from your community network. This is harder to do if you are tutoring college or adult students since geographically clients will be harder to come by, unless you are in a college town.

Going solo is likely the better route if you are tutoring for full-time income as well, as you will keep more revenue in your pocket. Additionally, recordkeeping / collecting payments will not seem overbearing if it is your full-time business.

Pros of Working With a Service:

- Hassle-free advertising. These services help you find more clients from more places

- Dispute resolution and issue mediation

- Payment collection, tax reporting, and basic record-keeping (hours, students, fees, etc.)

- Tool usage. Many providers now have their own platforms to utilize whiteboards and other digital experience tools. Some of these are very complex with formula editors, the ability to save your work and send it to the student as well as allowing both the tutor and student to use the whiteboard or canvas simultaneously.

Cons of Working With a Service:

- The service will likely take a commission from your fee (and it may be substantial)

- May have a minimum hour commitment per week or month

- May require certain credentials or education levels

- Some have set materials or outlines they require the tutor to use

- You cannot always choose who you work with, even if it is not a good fit (it is not always easy to decline students with services, or you may be penalized if you do so)

One often overlooked con of working with a service is becoming financially reliant on that service. If 50% or more of your business comes from one website or partner service, consider what would happen if they shut down their operations or changed their fee structure. Just because a company has been in business for years does not mean they cannot shut down tomorrow. Keep this in mind as you consider the sources of your clients.

The choice to go solo or work with a service is an important one. Personally, I have found a good mix between the two, usually by starting with clients sourced from a service, who then recommend friends and family to me as a solo tutor.

Setting Up a Business

Note: This chapter generally applies only to tutors charging for services

Setting up an official business is another critical decision point for a tutor. By setting up an official business I mean either incorporating or creating a Limited Liability Company (LLC) (or similar government-recognized business entity). If you are tutoring as a full-time job, hiring other tutors to work with you, or want to use a business name other than your own name, creating a recognized business is a logical step to ensure compliance with laws and protect your assets.

A pro and con list of setting up a business is presented for your consideration. You will find there are many pros, and it is something I encourage for anyone looking to create a tutoring business.

Pros of Setting Up a Business:

- It is easier to separate your personal income and expenses from your tutoring business income and expenses. This is incredibly helpful come tax time.

- May provide limited liability. As the name suggests, many organizations are formed as Limited Liability Companies or Limited Liability Corporations. These organizations provide their owners limited liability for certain business events (check with an attorney if you have questions) and can protect the owner from loss of personal assets in some situations.

- Ability to use a trade name other than your personal name. Some states and municipalities require an official application to operate a business under a trade name, which is sometimes called a "doing business as" (DBA) name. Applying for an LLC or other entity may open this door, potentially helping your business gain legitimacy. Personally, I have had an LLC for many years and have offered my services through my LLC name since it adds a level of credibility.

- Discounts and business-only subscriptions. Having a small business may mean opportunities to open business banking accounts, obtain volume discounts from retailers, and possibly discounts on utilities.

- Ability to join the local chamber of commerce or other professional associations. Some of these organizations and associations require a formal business to join and this may help you network and gain access to more clients.

Some (But Minimal) Cons of Setting Up an Official Business

- It costs money. The charge will vary by state, but most are a few hundred dollars per year.

- Some services will not allow you to provide services under a trade name. This usually is not a problem but can feel like a waste if you do not use the business name for anything else.

- It is extra time and paperwork. There are annual filing requirements, address updating, and recertifications which vary from state to state.

Are You Sure You Are Not Setting Up a Business?

While you may not think that meeting with a student or two during the week at your house is a true business, your local or state laws may say otherwise. Many cities and towns have home occupation permits, tax certificates, and other requirements if you plan on operating a business out of your home.

I Am Not Tutoring Students in Person. Do I Still Need a License?

Surprisingly, you might. In one of my former locations, I needed both a home occupation permit and a business license tax certificate to operate my online tutoring business. I never had clients at my home, but my jurisdiction required it.

Tutoring Policies

Once you have decided if you are going solo or signing up with a service, the next step is to write down your tutoring policies. Keep in mind if you utilize a partner service, they may have a set of their own policies that both you and your prospective students must abide by. You may be able to supplement these, but they will supersede any additional terms you have while using the partner service.

- **Session cancelation, late starts, and no-show policies.** These policies are critical to ensure an understanding of how valuable time is (even if you are providing your tutoring for free). Your policies may be restrictive depending on how many students you have, where your session is taking place, and how much (if anything) you are charging. When I first started, I was relatively generous with my policies to acquire more students. However, a few late cancels and no-shows to lessons where I was not able to find another student to fill the time made me reconsider. In general, I have found an 8–12-hour cancelation policy sufficient for tutors working for free or as a part-time job. Twenty-four hours may be more reasonable if you are a full-time tutor counting on tutoring income. I usually charge a penalty equal to 50% of the expected session fee if a student cancels late. A late cancel is where the student cancels before the session starts but inside the cancelation hour window established. When a student does not show within the first 10 minutes of the scheduled lesson start, I charge the full session even if the student shows after this time. It is up to you how long you want to wait around for a student to show, depending if you are online or in a physical location.

- o **Key Point: Do NOT change your policies after you have started with a student and do NOT have multiple policies. Once you set up a policy, stick to it without exception. Doing so will ensure things are fair and simple for you and your students.**

- **Payment terms and methods**: If you are charging for your services, you want your payment terms to be clear and consistent. Do NOT tutor on credit. I expect students to pay for a session either before it takes place or before the next one is scheduled. If the student does not pay within 24 hours of a lesson completion, then you should cancel any future scheduled lessons until the balance is paid. You will quickly find out that letting a payment slide once will turn into twice and more.

For payment methods, there are a variety of options to utilize:

- o Cash. Cash always works, but few students or parents have cash on hand, and you might need to have change on hand if your prices are not in increments of 20 dollars. You will also need to make repeated trips to the bank if you do not want to keep a lot of cash lying around.

- o Checks: I am not a big fan of checks because you run the risk of one of them bouncing (meaning the account does not have enough money to cover the check), but if you have been working with a client for a while, it is an option, and most banks have mobile deposit to save you a trip to the bank.

- o Venmo, PayPal, Zelle: All good options, although depending on your volume you may need to register as a business to utilize them.

- o Credit Card: I personally do not take credit cards, but if you are doing a large volume and do not mind paying some fees, it might be worth getting a product that would allow you to take credit cards with a mobile device.

- **Academic honesty, scope of services provided**: Unfortunately, even with all the attention paid over the years to cheating scandals, plagiarized papers, and crowdsourced exam solutions, cheating and academic dishonesty are still prevalent. It must be made clear to the student that not only will you not assist with any assignment where help is not permitted, but that knowledge of any such academic dishonesty will be reported to the student's academic institution. Fortunately, I haven't had to take this step, but there have been times I have been contacted by a student willing to pay (often a very large) sum of money to "do an assignment," "give them an answer," or "take this test with them." There is no grey area here. Doing a student's work for them is never acceptable.

- However, in other cases there are some grey areas, and they vary by subject and type of work. Helping a student through a difficult homework assignment or practice set may be acceptable, assuming it is not timed, and you are in fact "assisting" and not "doing." In addition to being unethical, doing a student's work for them does the student no favors as they are unlikely to learn the material if you are doing it for them.

- When in doubt, err on the side of caution and kindly decline engagements that may lead to this type of conflict. If you find yourself in this situation, kindly remind the student of the policies you set up at the start about academic honesty.

- **Session Particulars**: This section covers any other piece of relevant information you want to communicate to students prior to their first session. For example, do you expect the student to bring their own materials (textbooks, assignments, sports equipment, etc.), or will you provide that for them? How long do you hold each session? Do you allow for sessions to be recorded? These policies should be written down and presented to the student prior to the first lesson.

PART TWO

PRICING & FINDING STUDENTS

Market Research

Before you decide how much you are going to charge, it is important to determine the size of the market and the potential demand for your services. There are a few ways to figure this out, with a key difference between online and in-person tutoring.

For In-Person Tutoring

A few ideas to determine the size of your market:

- If you are working with elementary, middle, or high school students, search for the size of the schools in the geographic area you are considering or call the local board of education to determine the school system's size (how many students are in each grade).

    o Do not forget to count private or religious schools as well.

- If you are working with college students, determine the size of the colleges and universities in the geographic area. If possible, browse around the websites of these locations to see if you can get a feeling for the size of the programs with courses you might tutor.

    o There are a lot of private and public colleges, so ensure your search includes all institutions within the area you are covering.

- For all other categories, general population in your target range will help to initially size the opportunity. If you can find the percent of the population within your target age, that will provide an even better estimate.

For Online Tutoring

- If you are working solo, you will need to do a lot of digging to get this information. This might include searching job boards for tutor postings or searching the net for your subject(s) of expertise.

  - Try searching for "(insert subject) tutors." If there are a good number of results, it is likely that there is a strong demand. However, just because you do not see a lot of offerings, it may mean you are one of the first to serve this market.

- Even if you are not utilizing a partner or sourcing service, you can still usually search these types of sites to see if there are posts requesting tutors in a particular subject.

- If you are utilizing partner programs or referral services, you can usually see the entire listing of postings for jobs by subject area.

  - On some sites, you may also be able to see how many other tutors there are in the same subjects, and occasionally the rate they charge, which can help price your services competitively.

Once you have determined the size of the market, you need to narrow the results to those who may be interested in your services.

If you are tutoring in person, there are a few opportunities to research this:

- If you are a parent or know parents of students in the age range you are focusing on, ask around. Do these students need help in the subjects you focus on? Does the name of a particular tutor or educational center continue to pop up? What about them is drawing business? These questions can help to size the local market.

- Search social media sites that focus on the local area such as Nextdoor, Patch.com, and local Facebook groups. Occasionally you will see discussions around certain classes, or even solicitations for help.

- Visit local coffee shops and libraries. You may find advertisements for other tutors and services giving you an idea of what is in the market currently in your area.

- Sometimes, there may be a local education or community fair where vendors may be present. You may want to check these out to see if a lot of tutoring services are present and if their booths are attended.

If you are tutoring online, research can be somewhat easier:

- If you are using a partner service, you can usually see how many students are looking for help in the subjects you cover.

- For solo tutors, you might be able to solicit feedback through online polls or surveys. If you search "free survey responses," there are many avenues to get responses. However, keep in mind these are generally not scientific and often lead to a lot of people saying they would be interested but really are not serious and would not actually pay.

- Similar to in-person research, ask around your social network or use your social media network to determine who might be interested in your services.

Pricing

Before you find your first student, you will need to figure out how much to charge for your services. If you are looking to tutor pro-bono (free), feel free to skip this section.

What to charge depends on a variety of factors (there are entire books on how to price services) but a few main ones you should consider:

- The subject matter you are teaching. If you have a specialty in which there are few tutors (see market research topic above), you can charge a premium for your services. That said, you may not be able to price at a premium until you prove your success in this area with a few positive reviews and logged hours.

- Delivery method. In-person lessons (unless done at your home), should always cost more than similar online lessons. I generally charge a 25%-50% premium for lessons in which I need to travel to a student's location. The reason for this is two-fold. First, you must consider the cost of gas, parking, and the potential coffee you would buy if you met at a public location; Second, if it takes you 30 minutes to reach a student for a 60-minute lesson, and 30 minutes to get back home, the lesson "time" is really two hours, not an hour. When working with students online or back-to-back at the same location, you can easily move from one to the next with only a quick 5-minute bathroom break.

- Type of student: this is more difficult because in certain areas, parents may be picking up the tab for their child. You must consider the region (and if online, the general competition rate) you are working in and the clientele you are serving. Cities where demand is high and high-income areas may allow you to price your services at a premium.

- o This is another benefit of tutoring online if you are in a lower-income area. While students locally may only be able to afford a rate of X, it is likely you will find students online who will pay well over that rate.

- Your experience, reputation, and skill level: If you are highly experienced and reading this book to improve on your current offerings, then your service price should reflect this. If you are a five-star tutor on a website with a few hundred hours of tutoring under your belt and a bunch of great reviews, factor this into your price. Finally, as you would with any other job, if you hold credentials, academic honors, or other titles that would make your tutoring more valuable, include those in your price consideration as well.

  - o If you are just starting out, consider pricing your services a little lower than the competition to attract business. However, be careful not to price yourself too low where the student might read you as being cheap and inexperienced.

- Commissions and other expenses: If you are working with a partner service, there will likely be a fee (and sometimes a sizable one), for referrals of students, or possibly on each lesson provided. Keep this in mind when setting your rate. It is easy to charge $50 an hour and quickly realize you are actually taking home $35 after commission.

- Other expenses: There are a variety of other expenses you will incur as a tutor (a detailed description of how to track these expenses are covered later):

  o For all tutors: Consider the cost of educational materials, textbooks, and supplies (refer back to the "Materials" section earlier in the book)

  o For in-person tutors: Consider the cost of gas, tolls, and parking, if applicable

  o For online tutors: Consider internet expenses and any computer software or hardware

  o Taxes: This is an often-overlooked area. If you are a self-employed person in the United States, you will be paying income tax as well as the Self Employment Tax. As of 2022, the self-employment tax was 15.3%. Between this tax and the income tax, a significant piece of your rate will be put towards this area.

  o Retirement and Health Insurance: Remember that if this is your full-time business, a comparable job might contribute to a retirement account and chip in for health insurance, so this needs to be covered unless a family member's plan covers you.

- Opportunity Cost: This is a very personal decision, but if tutoring is not your full-time job, then you need to think about what you are giving up to be a tutor. If you are missing your kid's basketball game to tutor (seriously consider if that is the best use of your time), then the rate you charge should reflect this. If you are missing an hour of sleep or an hour of your favorite TV show, the rate should reflect that as well. On the other hand, if you really enjoy tutoring (which you should!) and find pleasure in seeing students do well, then your cost should reflect your satisfaction in providing services.

I have seen tutors charge as low as $20-$25 an hour, and some very specialized exam tutors charge near $300 per hour. The average rate in your area can vary greatly, so use the "market research" tips above to best price your services.

A quick note about variable pricing. I am a big proponent of charging different rates to different students, but it must be done carefully. The decision to charge one student more than another must be an ethical one and not based on personal preference or any other arbitrary reason. I have priced students higher if they want to meet during what I consider premium hours (e.g., weekends or late evenings). I have also charged more if the lessons require more time than average to prepare for, or if the subject the student is working on is very challenging.

As a practical example, I have charged $60+ per hour for many of my undergraduate financial accounting students, but $100+ per hour for those studying the Certified Public

Accountant (CPA) exam. The CPA exam requires much more effort on my part to prepare for the lessons, keep up with the material (the exam changes), and is, in general, a more difficult topic. Intro classes hardly change, and generally do not require much prep time, given my experience working with them.

You might also change your rate depending on the season and your activity level. For college tutors, the summer months tend to be very slow, as does the holiday season into January. During these periods, I reduce my rate to pick up students who may be taking a shorter summer class or preparing for a fall class but are not willing to spend as much.

Advertising and Securing Students

Now that you have identified the potential market and set your prices and policies, it is time to start looking for students. There are a variety of ways I have sourced clients over the years.

At first, marketing and advertising can be one of the most challenging parts of starting your business. Most tutors do not get into their businesses to gain experience with selling activities, but after time this part of running your business will become easier. One of the best ways to acquire new students is from existing and former students, so as you grow your business, you will find that students will start to come to you rather than you having to reach them.

Depending on your budget and if you are tutoring full or part-time, your need and desire to advertise services will vary. For those tutoring part-time, free options may secure the number of clients you are looking for. If you are looking to build a full-time business, you will likely need to put some money towards paid advertising options.

Free Options

- If you are working with a partner service, this is one of the biggest benefits. They do most of, if not all, the advertising and promotion for you. Your profile will appear in the results, and they will advertise their service or site through different methods. Keep in mind that the partner may rank you based on your rate, experience, or credentials, so be sure to keep them up-to-date.

- Local tutor options that are free include putting flyers at local coffee shops, community bulletin boards, schools (assuming it is allowed/approved), or libraries (again, if allowed and approved).

- Join and post your service on appropriate Facebook and local social networking sites (Nextdoor.com is one I have seen a few promotions on).

- Communicate with your in-person and social networks about your new business. Make sure to be specific about the type of students and subjects you are covering.

- Your religious institution, local chamber of commerce, or other organizations may have a free area to promote your business.

- Do not forget, word of mouth always works, so always keep business cards on hand and ready!

A Few Words About Flyers and Posters

You can search the internet for templates of tutoring flyers, but these are some pro tips that will ensure you get the best results:

- Include an up-to-date headshot of yourself in professional attire (try to smile!)

- Use a QR code (usually free) so that students can scan your flyer with their smartphone

- List out all subjects you cover

- List your experience and qualifications (but do not overwhelm the page)

- Do NOT put rates on the flyer (many reasons why, but primarily if the rates change you do not want to have to go replace them)

- I have mixed emotions about tear-off tabs (perforations) that contain the business name, cell phone number, and email. I prefer QR codes as they look more professional and 21st century, but you may want to try both.

- Use higher quality, heavier stock paper. You can get good results from higher quality at-home printers, or you may try an office printing store.

Paid Options

I generally do not recommend paying for advertising unless you are making tutoring your full-time business, or you have had minimal success using free methods. These costs quickly add up, and if you do not source students from them, it is very frustrating.

- Google, Facebook, Twitter, or YouTube ads. Generally, these work best for online tutors, but you can target location-specific areas as well, though it may cost you more.

- Sponsorship of a local event such as a golf outing or charity road race. I have never tried this, but many small businesses have had success getting clients through these events, which can be helpful in a local market.

- Direct mail. You can send direct mail to local clients, but this is only recommended for full-time tutors with a good in-person location.

- Website promotion. If you have a website up and running, you can purchase ads and clicks to drive traffic to the website, and hopefully secure clients through there. You may also want to consider search engine optimization (SEO) which can help your website rank higher in search results, especially with your target audience.

PART THREE

THE LESSONS

Congrats! You have found your first student. The following section takes you step-by-step through the next phase in your tutoring journey.

Before the First Lesson

Even before the first session starts, it is essential to set expectations with a new student. After a while, these ground rules and policies may become part of your everyday process when working with a new student. To a new student, setting these expectations and understanding them will give reassurance that the tutor is prepared and the first, and subsequent lessons, will run efficiently and effectively.

In the previous section (setting your policies), you wrote down some of your essential policies regarding your tutoring services. Now is the time to communicate these to your student, and their parents if applicable. In addition to these policies, there are a few other things I like to communicate prior to the first meeting:

- Ask the student to come to the first meeting early. It makes things a lot easier if you can start even 5 minutes early (at no charge to the student), to go through pleasantries, as well as give a short buffer if the student has trouble getting to the physical location or struggling with online technologies or connectivity.

- Expectations: Discuss what the student is to bring to the first session including lesson materials, textbooks, etc. vs. what you will provide to them.

- Academic honesty reminder: Clearly communicate that while you will do what you can to help them, working on exams or doing work for them will not happen.

- Cancelation reminder: Ensure the student is aware of any late, no-show, or cancelation policies you provided earlier.

- Comfort reminder: Now is also a good time to remind the student that the time is theirs, and they should feel free to dress comfortably and, if applicable, use a webcam.

- Payment: Ask how the student intends to pay for the session whether that is a check, a credit card, or cash so you can prepare. This is also a good reminder for the student that payment is due at the time of service unless you have planned otherwise.

- Information check: Ensure the student has directions to the tutoring location if needed, the time of the session is confirmed and they have the appropriate link and password if needed to connect to an online lesson if you are tutoring online.

After reminding the student of these policies, it is a good time to review materials the student has sent to you. This can be anything from a cursory read (assuming you are familiar with the material), to practicing problems, and making notes. Your notes may even turn into a lesson plan outline. It will be quickly apparent to the student if you have not read or at least considered what materials they want to cover. After the first lesson, this exercise becomes easier as you can judge the students' abilities and comprehension.

There is one last item that some tutors choose to utilize which is a tutoring services agreement. This is a contract that provides key policy points with respect to your tutoring arrangement. Personally, I always use a tutoring services agreement in case of a dispute with a student where there is an official document to reference. I include my payment policies, a brief description of the service being provided and what is not provided. I also note that I will not disclose records to any outside party unless the client gives permission to do so, or it is required by law. I ask the client to sign a copy and return it to me, and then I will sign a copy and return it to the client for their records.

Some tutors may find this too formal, and some clients may shy away from signing an agreement. However, keep in mind that in business, what is written is easier to prove. A tutoring service agreement will help keep all parties aware of the arrangement parameters and can be referred to later if there are any questions. There are sample templates online, or, reach out to me (contact information provided at the end of the book) and I will gladly provide one.

The First Lesson

Aside from the pre-first lesson activities, the first minutes of the initial tutoring session are the most critical. These moments can change the entire course of your working relationship. The first few minutes of this lesson can result in securing a life-long client, or conversely, facing an unhappy student never to be heard from again.

There are a few critical key points in preparation for this time to remind yourself when working with a new client. After you have been tutoring for a while, it is easy to fall into a sense of security and brush these activities aside, but they must not be ignored. This is likely the first time the student is meeting you, and first impressions are lasting impressions. Also, keep in mind that for some students this may be the first time they have ever been tutored before. This could mean the student is shy, embarrassed, or potentially even angry. By setting the right tone in the early moments, you are more likely to be successful with your tutoring.

Starting the First Lesson

- Do not be late. The first lesson sets the standard for all future lessons. If you are late the first time, the student will assume you are late all the time and that your time, and theirs, is not valuable. Being late in the event of an emergency is sometimes unavoidable, but you should make every effort to start the first meeting on time, if not early, as discussed before.

- Have any materials the student has sent to you ready to go, or textbooks at the ready. If you do not have at least some knowledge of what the student is looking to cover during their sessions with you, then you as the tutor have failed to do your homework. In this case, I would strongly suggest going back to the prior chapter and reviewing the "before the first lesson" tips.

- Do not rush right into the material. It is important to at least have a few moments of "get-to-know-you" time before diving into the lesson topics. However, do not spend half your time going through your background and engaging in meaningless small talk. You want the student to feel comfortable with you, but since they hired you, they likely already know the key points of your background and experience, and you do not need to know their life story.

- Walk through BOTH the student's preferred learning style (verbal, visual, hands-on) and your experience with delivering the subject content. Usually, it is the tutor's responsibility to be flexible and adapt to the student's preferred learning style. However, as we'll discuss in the next section, it is okay to try different approaches to materials, if the student is open to it.

During the First Lesson

The first lesson will tell you a lot about a student, their learning style, and their current level of comfort with the subject matter. You may also pick up information about the student's personality which can help in making them feel comfortable and also give insight into when something may be bothering a student. There are a few things I try to observe about the student during the first session which will help to prepare and adapt for future sessions. In no particular order:

- Is the student prepared for the lesson, and do they have questions they wish to cover? If not, do you find yourself doing a lot of handholding to determine areas for improvement and spending time trying to determine what the student wants to study?

  - Remember that some students may not want to admit what they do not know or what they are struggling with, so it is important to ensure that you are encouraging and welcoming all questions and areas of confusion.

  - If the student seems to be disorganized, it may be an indication that a lack of focus could be contributing to any learning difficulty. When I see a student struggling with organization, I offer a few tips. Taking thorough notes and putting materials into folders organized by date or subject area are some of my favorite suggestions to start with. Also, it helps to be more direct with these students. This means when assigning homework or preparations for the next session, specify material to work on rather than suggesting the student look through questions they do not understand. Chances are the student will be better served if you provide specific instructions such as "work on problems 3, 5 and 15" or "repeat the pronunciation of that word" instead of "practice the material."

- If a student comes to you at the middle or end of the semester or academic year, it is important to quickly assess where the student is with material that has already been covered in the course. This may even require considering the student's prior academic background in the subject.

  - Typically, when students come to me at the middle or end of a semester or school year, I find that they are missing critical pieces of foundational information. This may be painful, and sometimes costly, but in certain instances, you have to go back to the beginning. If a student comes with struggles in more advanced topics, test their foundational knowledge first. If that is solid, you know it is a topical problem rather than a foundational problem. However, if the student is struggling with foundations, then you need to encourage review and mastery of those concepts before moving on.

- Does the student struggle with certain types of problems, or is there a particular part of their course that is giving them trouble? Sometimes a student may be good at math, but their reading comprehension is lacking, which would show itself in word problems. Occasionally you might find the student is grasping the subject but is having trouble with technology, such as a calculator. On the other hand, I have seen students who are great writers, but cannot spell and then becoming embarrassed and push off assignments requiring writing skills.

Learning Styles

- There are many different types of learners. Some students like to hear you speak and will write down their own notes, while others will want to see everything step by step written down. In the first session, I like to ask the student what type of learning style they believe works best for them and take that into account. That said, sometimes you will find a student who claims they are a visual learner, but having the student read back their own work to you provides greater benefit. Consider this, trying different approaches is the best idea in the early lessons so you can see if the student adapts or responds well to a particular method over another. There is a balance between adapting to a student's request and choosing the method that works best for them. Ultimately, they are your client, and you should strive to make them happy, but not at the expense of their education. If there seems to be a disconnect, point out an example where another method has been tried and the student succeeded. Doing so may provide an opportunity for the student to see how beneficial the alternative method is.

- The Socratic method involves asking questions repeatedly until the students provide a response. This is one of my favorite tools to determine a student's learning style in the initial meeting. Some students will be shy and may not provide an answer even if they know it. This is incredibly helpful information for you as the tutor. If the student does not respond to coaxing, do not push. Over time, confidence can be gained and you can try again. I also like the Socratic method to determine if students think they have the right answer or path forward when, in reality, they are working with flawed logic. In many cases, I have found the student believes they are doing something correctly, and this confidence is actually causing a problem. Instead, have the student consider other approaches or fact patterns.

Ending Your First Lesson

- Always end your lessons on a positive note. Leaving a session with a student feeling defeated, confused, or annoyed is a sure way for them to not want to come to the next lesson (and if you are being reviewed, do not expect a positive mark).

- Even if the student is struggling, always provide encouraging words and ensure the student that it takes time to learn anything. However, do not claim that "it will get easier" or make other false promises. Learning anything takes hard work, and the student must remember that success will only come with their involvement and commitment.

- If possible, highlight something during the session that the student did well, especially if it related to a prior lesson or work the student did on their own. This will reinforce the student's confidence and show them you are paying attention to their progress.

- Do not leave any open ends with regards to scheduling, payment, etc. The student should either know when the next lesson is (if applicable) or leave a few minutes at the end to discuss scheduling. Remember, failing to plan is planning to fail.

- Now is a good time to remind the student of any assignments, review problems, readings, etc. that were discussed during the lesson for them to bring next time. If the student forgot to bring something to the lesson or needs to bring something specific to the next lesson, ensure they leave the lesson knowing what to bring next time.

The Second and Future Lessons

Starting Lessons

It is always a good idea to start a session by asking the student if they need clarification on anything from the prior lesson. I like to ask this up front, as it is more likely the student will forget about the question as the lesson goes on. If you assigned the student homework or something to practice, I would recommend starting the session by asking about this. Again, it highlights that you have paid attention to the student and they will feel accountable to you.

During Lessons

Now is a good time to revisit your initial assessment of the student's learning style and organizational abilities. As the number of sessions increase, you might revise your initial assessment, or confirm what you first thought.

Depending on how the student responds to the initial sessions, you may want to try different teaching methods to see if the student responds well to presenting material in a different format. Of course, if the student is doing well with the subject matter, then there might not be a reason to change your approach. During subsequent lessons, I also like to gather feedback from students on what they think is working, or not working, with the tutoring program. Do they find you are being too quick or too slow explaining material? Do they want additional practice exercises or more detailed notes? Likely, you will already have an idea about the progress of your tutoring, but I have found it beneficial to check in with the student from time to time to ensure my observations are correct. Plus, this will give you a chance to address any opportunities to strengthen your tutoring skills.

Wrapping Up Subsequent Lessons

Just as you did after the first lesson, it is important to give or send digitally any notes or saved whiteboard work or edits to the student. It is best to do this immediately at the end of the lesson or as you are wrapping up. It is likely you will forget later, and the student may need the information for an upcoming exam or paper.

At the end of a tutoring arrangement with a student, or perhaps at the end of a semester, take the opportunity to ask the student for a written review. If you have a website or use a partner service that allows for reviews, see if your student will provide a public testimonial. Many will if they are happy, and hopefully they are, with the service you have provided them, and this is a great way to prove your worth to future students. Ask the student to be specific about the types of instruction provided and the results. It is a great opportunity to showcase your efforts to help students achieve higher grades or test scores.

Preparing for Exams

Over the years I have worked with dozens of students seeking out help in preparation for an exam or quiz. Many tutors are familiar with large standardized tests used for college entrance exams or for advanced class testing, but if you are not tutoring these topics, most exam prep will be routine class quizzes and tests.

When getting ready for exams, the content is, of course, the most critical aspect of preparation. However, tutors should also consider:

- Is the exam timed, and if so, how does the student do under time pressure?

- Is the exam multiple choice, written short answer, essay format, or a combination?

- Does the student get points for showing their work? If so, emphasize this in lessons.

- Can the student go back to previous parts of the exam if time allows?

- Where is the student going to take the exam i.e., classroom, home, other location? The student should feel comfortable in that setting, so walk them through this.

An often-overlooked area is the student's mindset while preparing for an exam. Some of my best and brightest students were terrible test takers. Simply put, their anxiety got the best of them. They knew the material well and had spent adequate time preparing, but choked during test time.

During a session immediately prior to a quiz or exam, I like to leave a few extra minutes to go through the student's mindset. Do they think they can pass the exam? Are they nervous or stressed? If you think the student is experiencing pre-test anxiety, there are a few tips that my students have found helpful:

- Remind the student that having a positive mindset has been linked to greater success on exams and academic endeavors. In other words, if the student believes they will do well, they have a better chance of that outcome.

- Breathing exercises. I routinely have to remind myself to take a few deep breaths while sitting in traffic or when I get annoyed at work. Deep breathing with a few slow breaths is helpful for students to get in the right mindset before starting a test.

- Students may feel like one test will make or break their entire academic career, class, or semester. While some tests do have a lot of weight and carry a significant portion of grades, the tutor should remind the student that it is not a life-or-death situation. This can help the student remember that no matter what, as long as they do their best, things will work out in the end.

Reviewing for Exams

Even if an exam or quiz went well, it is worth reviewing the results with the student. If an exam went well, the tutor should ask the student how they felt going into the exam and point out the hard work the student put in to getting the grade. This highlights for the student the value of their efforts, making them more likely to prepare in the same way for the next exam. This can also help increase a student's confidence moving forward.

If an exam goes poorly, you must balance between spending time reviewing the exam and paying too much time and attention dwelling on the outcome. Reviewing a bad exam with a student can be a difficult point in the tutoring relationship. In some cases, the student may feel that you did not prepare them adequately for the exam. I like to take the following approach:

Root Cause Discovery

- Was the student adequately prepared and did they put sufficient time into reviewing the material?

    o If not, this is an opportunity to stress the level of time commitment needed by the student outside of tutoring lessons. Consider other preparation methods such as simulated exams and additional homework that may help the student next time.

- Did the format of the exam cause issues for the student?

- o Review how the exam was structured and keep this in mind for future exam preparations. Was the student timed, did they have the ability to go between questions, or were they forced to move on once an answer was submitted? Was it a multiple-choice test, or was the student required to write their work out?

- If the student was adequately prepared, did they have the right mindset entering the test?

  - o What caused the student to have anxiety or other mental blocks during the exam? Was there a stressful situation at home or school causing outside stress? Perhaps the student thought they would not do well and that translated into a poor performance?

- Did you adequately prepare them and provide correct information during your sessions?

  - o This is a hard self-reflection moment as a tutor, but it must be done. Students who had been working with other tutors sometimes bring me exam results with incorrect equations, flawed logic, and bad explanations. After review, it was clear they had been tutored incorrectly. If you review an exam and find out you made a mistake in instructing the student, you must evaluate your qualifications again. Honest mistakes are bound to happen, but repeated errors by the tutor in instruction are not acceptable.

It does not matter if the student got a 100 or a 0 on a test. It is the tutor's job to encourage and support and use all tools available to continue success or ensure it for the next time.

PART FOUR

RUNNING YOUR BUSINESS

After a few short months, I found myself being comfortable with the pace and approach of tutoring. As you settle into a rhythm with tutoring, it is important to ensure you are monitoring the health of your business. A few quick check-ins are worth revisiting in some areas:

Periodic Reviews of your Business

- Are you keeping accurate financial records? If not, you may want to look at either small business bookkeeping software, or potentially hiring a part-time bookkeeper.

- Do you find yourself not having time for anything else but tutoring? If so, check out the "Expanding Your Business" section below.

- Is the space you are tutoring in conducive to the volume of students you have now?

- What early successes or failures have you found? What about those situations can you replicate, or perhaps avoid, as you continue?

- If you haven't been as successful as you have wanted, this is also an opportunity to visit your rate and subjects. Be careful with changing rates in either direction, since your current students will inevitably find out and may ask you to lower your rate (if you lowered it for others). If you raised your rate, your current students may ask you to keep their rate the same as it has been.

- Continue to promote your business through your new network of clients, revisiting any advertising strategies or campaigns you have run successfully.

- Now is a great time to set up a website if you do not have one already. If you do have a website, update it with success stories and/or client testimonials.

Be honest with yourself when it comes to revenue and expenses. Are you charging enough to cover your costs? If this is your full-time business, have you factored in items like health insurance, retirement savings, and income taxes? If this is a part-time job, are you sacrificing your full-time work or other obligations to tutor?

Common Pitfalls and Difficult Situations

- **Taking on too many students**: This problem may seem like a nice one to have, especially if you are just starting out and looking for your first few clients. As you progress, especially if you are a good tutor, you will find yourself getting a lot of requests. Being busy is fine, but be careful if you find yourself overscheduling. If you are constantly having to reschedule students or are not able to accommodate a core few clients on a regular basis, you might be taking on too many clients. If you are struggling to keep up with student demand, revisit your list from the Getting Started chapter where you wrote down the subjects, type of students, and skill level you planned to focus on. Have you stuck to those, or do you find yourself consistently out of your lane, perhaps working on subjects you might not be well versed in? Now is a good time to re-assess and perhaps revise your current client list.

- **Safety and Security**: In today's world, safety and security mean a lot more. Let us state the obvious. Never put yourself, a student, or anyone or anything in an uncomfortable situation. If you find yourself uncomfortable working with a student, end the tutoring relationship.

- **Working with children**: If you are working with young children, you must ensure that both the child and their responsible party are comfortable if you work with them alone. In addition, I highly recommend you channel all communications through the adult when dealing with children, especially those under the age of 13. Older children may have their own cell phone or e-mail, but you should always copy their responsible adult in any communications. I cannot stress this enough. Children have a different view of the world, and what may seem like an innocent remark, joke, or comment could be taken many ways. Always keep your communications professional and use direct statements rather than implied thoughts or sentiments.

- **Working with people your age**: Although I am older now than when I first started tutoring, in the early days I was only a few years older (and in some cases younger!) than the person I was tutoring. This can lead to a potentially uncomfortable scenario if you are not careful. The buddy scenario is exactly as it sounds...you become friends with the student. There is nothing wrong with making a solid personal connection; however, you need to ensure that during your tutoring relationship, there is a clear delineation between the "friend" time and the "work" time. Generally, the best way to avoid this problem is to set a clear "get to work" time where only topics related to material are allowed. Alternatively, if you find your student is interested in a "non-tutoring relationship" with you, you must make it clear that it is unacceptable during the duration of the tutoring agreement. If it comes to it, you should not be afraid to end the relationship.

- **Working "non-tech savvy" people**: This can either be a fun or a very frustrating problem to have (this could be one of the topics you tutor!). Especially if you are attempting to tutor a student online, make sure the student has the appropriate background knowledge to access the system or systems you are utilizing, and, if needed, perform a technical "setup" meeting ahead of your first tutoring session. This will help ensure the first lesson will be focused on the subject matter, not the setup of a computer.

- **Working with people from different cultures**: One of the perks of being a tutor, especially if you offer online lessons, is getting to meet people from all over the world. It is important to be cognizant of cultural differences when working with others, especially when providing feedback in the form of constructive criticism. In some cultures, you may find that students are more sensitive to certain phrases or terms. If you are unsure about working with someone from a particular background, a quick internet search will be helpful. Alternatively, you can politely ask if there are any items the student might want you to know about with respect to their background.

- **Payment Problems**: This is an easy problem to avoid if you set expectations with the student up front. There should be no uncertainty about how, when, and how much a student is expected to pay for your tutoring services. One of the best things you can do is to never tutor on credit. This means you will not schedule another session with a student until they have paid for the last one. Many a tutor has gotten in trouble after they have worked with a student who has paid consistently over time, and then they forget once... and then twice... and soon they are behind four or five sessions. Your focus as a tutor is to tutor, not spend time chasing payments. Make your payment policies and methods clear to students from the start, and you can avoid this problem entirely.

Expanding Your Business

In this chapter, we discuss the problem most tutors face, especially those that are charging for their tutoring. This is growing your tutoring business.

Let us face it, there are only 24 hours in a day. Even if tutoring is your full-time job, you probably will not work more than 60 hours a week, assuming you are covering weekends. This leads a lot of tutors to do one of the following:

- Abandon all social life activities

- Ignore family, friends, spouses, and other commitments

- Increase their fee amount, potentially losing clients

- Burn out

None of the above are ideal situations to be in. What can be done?

- Work with multiple students concurrently. The easiest solution to the scale problem is to work with multiple students at the same time. There are a few best practices when applying this method:

  o Do not try to work with students at the same time if they are working on different subjects. The distraction for both the students and the tutor is too great.

- o If you are trying to move a 1:1 student to a group setting, ensure that the student you are working with is interested.

- o Even if the student is interested, would a multiple-student environment work well for them? Consider your student's needs, especially those with attention difficulties.

- o Ensure your rate reflects this. Generally, this is what appeals to students or parents. For example, you could charge $100/hr. for one-on-one tutoring, but $150/hr. for two students. You would make $50 an hour extra, and each student would save $25 per session...quite appealing!

- o There is a major caution with this method. Sometimes I have found that one student goes far ahead of the other with their comprehension of material, so much so that it may be a detriment for both students. In cases like this, you may want to speak with each student separately to see how they are feeling with the arrangement and if they are comfortable with the level being worked, if it is too easy or too hard. If needed, you may need to split the students to provide the best experience to both.

- Provide "non-live" tutoring. Many tutors I have spoken with will tell you that scheduling students is one of the hardest parts of administrating their business. Some subjects lend themselves to "non-live" tutoring, meaning the tutor provides guidance, but either through written or recorded delivery. Consider:

- o Proofreading, Excel sheet solutions, homework reviews, and even some math instruction can be provided with clear written directions

- o There are a lot of screen recording programs out there that will allow you to record yourself speaking while showing a step-by-step on your screen.

- Expand your offerings. Live tutoring is by far one of the best instructional methods to help students succeed, but there are other delivery options as well. Personally, I have explored the course platforms such as LinkedIn Learning, Udemy, and Teachable. These platforms either work with you to create content or allow you to put all your own content on their platforms. You might consider putting content on YouTube or selling flashcards or study guides that would supplement your in-person tutoring.

- Offer multi-session discounts if students book lessons in advance. In this situation, you will offer a discount anywhere from 10-25% if the client pays upfront and schedules the sessions in advance with you. This is incredibly helpful from a planning perspective for both time and financial management. If you know what revenue you have coming in as well as when students are scheduled, you can work your personal schedule and financial needs around this. This strategy also helps you retain clients longer, as paying for sessions up front will commit them to a longer-term relationship. Finally, this strategy reduces the number of payments you need to collect.

- One of my favorite ways to expand a tutoring business is to use an existing client base to find new students. The easiest way to do this is to offer current and/or former students a referral credit if a new student takes lessons with you. Be careful that the referral credit is not so lucrative that it outweighs the revenue from a new client. Generally, I offer a free lesson to a current student if their referral takes at least three sessions with me. If the referring person is not a current student, offer a gift card, preferably to a place you know the student would shop at, worth approximately the same as an hour session. This offers a good return, and also makes the student consider their referrals. The other caution is that your referral program should not become too complex. Remember, your job is tutoring, not running a promotional marketing firm. Finally, remember to record any gift cards or lesson discounts in your accounting records when applicable.

CONCLUSION

Throughout this book, the business of tutoring has been covered, from the initial "why do I want to tutor" question to expanding your business.

Tutoring can be enjoyed as a part-time job to supplement your full-time work, or it can be made into a full-time business. You can earn a respectable income, and all while helping students achieve their goals.

My favorite parts of tutoring are that I can define my own rates, choose my own clients, and set my own schedule. No matter if you choose to work with a partner organization or go completely solo, the flexibility of tutoring is appealing.

I hope this book has been helpful to you, sharing best practices as well as a step-by-step guide to start, grow, and maintain your business. While I anticipate these tips will be helpful, the most important thing I have found as a tutor is to bring passion, experience, and encouragement to every session with a student.

Finally, do not forget to keep up your own learning and development. As the world changes, there are new ways of doing things and new technologies to enable learning and content delivery. Ensure you are taking advantage of these methods to provide a great experience for your students.

Tutor on!

THE COMMANDMENTS OF TUTORING

1. Thou shall not tutor material without proper knowledge

2. Thou shall not put yourself or your student in an uncomfortable situation

3. Thou shall not tutor on credit

4. Thou shall not help a student cheat, do a student's homework, or write a student's paper

5. Thou shall keep accurate financial records

6. Thou shall keep the student's best interest in mind

7. Thou shall not burn out!

CONNECT WITH ME

I would love your feedback on this book, as well as to get connected professionally to understand some of your challenges (and successes!) as a tutor. You can reach me at pclancy@stratfieldsolutions.com, or visit my website, www.stratfieldsolutions.com

If you would really like to help me out, a quick review of this book on Amazon or a similar platform would go a long way and ensure other tutors are able to realize the benefits of the information contained within.

ACKNOWLEDGEMENTS

To God and the United States of America for giving me the opportunity to chase dreams.

To my parents for their support and editing help and to my entire family for encouragement.

To the faculty at The Catholic University of America, for providing the cornerstones of my knowledge, and the vision of how education can be used to serve others.

To the faculty at The George Washington University where I learned the importance of teamwork.

To my friend and fellow tutor Andrew Rudolphi for excellent feedback; and to Colin Howard for his keen eye.

To my former students turned lifelong friends, Chris Mayville, Elizabeth Deluca and Christina Howard.

Finally, but most importantly my students. Without them, I would not have been able to write this book. I have had amazing experiences working with students from all over the world. When people thought I was working a second job, I was really creating lifetime connections.

ABOUT THE AUTHOR

Patrick C. Clancy has tutored over 2,500 hours in a variety of subjects and is an active Certified Public Accountant (CPA) and Certified Fraud Examiner (CFE). He holds dual master's degrees (Business Administration and Accountancy) from the George Washington University (GWU) in Washington, D.C., and a bachelor's degree, Cum Laude, from the Catholic University of America (CUA) in Washington, D.C. At CUA, he was awarded the Wall Street Journal Student Achievement award in recognition of outstanding academic excellence and was elected Vice-President of the campus chapter of Pi Gamma Mu, the oldest interdisciplinary social science honor society. During his time at CUA he was a Teaching Assistant (TA) in the school of Business and Economics.

In 2013, Mr. Clancy founded Stratfield Strategic Solutions, LLC, a professional education and tutoring firm. In this capacity, he has reached over 250 students (and counting!), helping each to improve their skills in a variety of disciplines.

Mr. Clancy resides in his home state of Connecticut and is passionate about running, volleyball and travel (and of course, tutoring!)

www.ingramcontent.com/pod-product-compliance
Lightning Source LLC
Chambersburg PA
CBHW060035050426
42448CB00012B/3027